Rejected:
The Imperfect Accounting Student's Guide to Finding a Great Job and Life After College

Geoff Plourde, EA, CPA

Acknowledgements

The author wishes to thank the team at Aptus Press for their invaluable assistance in bringing this work from concept to publication and for the great deal of artistic license and control granted to the author, despite a great deal of weeping and gnashing of teeth resulting as a result of the author's exercise thereof.

DATE: 05 November 2017
TO: Current or Future Accounting Student
FROM: Geoff Plourde, EA, CPA
RE: This Book

You are probably asking yourself two questions right now.

1. What the hell is an imperfect accounting student?
2. Who the hell is this Geoff Plourde guy and what does he know about it?

Let's start with what an imperfect accounting student is.

An imperfect accounting student is an accounting student who has less than stellar grades and/or less than stellar interviewing skills.

Many larger accounting firms place a lot of emphasis on good grades and interviewing when hiring staff accountants. This means that if you don't make the cut, you don't get an interview or you don't get hired.

Some of you are probably wondering how I know this, but it's quite simple.

I once was an accounting student myself who had mediocre grades and mediocre interviewing skills.

I went to an accounting program where I watched many of my classmates with better grades and better charm get summer internships and offers from Big 4 and mid-tier firms before their senior year of college.

Unlike them, I started my senior year of college with no idea of where I would be working after college. It's kind of scary to realize graduation is 8 months away and you don't know what you're doing after. Even scarier if you have student loans that will soon come due.

Ironically, I ended up in a great job that had:

- ✓ a comfortable salary
- ✓ a consistent 40 hour workweek
- ✓ the flexibility to become a CPA, complete a tax practice fellowship, and go through graduate school.
- ✓ set me up to run a successful accounting practice after only two years

All this while my former classmates slaved away for 60 to 80 hours a week at their "great" job.

This book covers the process I went through to find this great job, get into grad school, and start my accounting practice, as well as information about things I wish I had done earlier that would have made finding a job easier.

I hope you find this information valuable and that it makes your life slightly easier.

Best wishes,

Geoff

Geoff Plourde, EA, CPA
geoff@gplourdecpa.com

Contents

Chapter 0: Where do I begin?

Key Concept:

Each chapter has a key concept or theme that I've placed up front to put the chapter in context and that I come back to at the end of most chapters. This chapter is about finding where to start in the book, as not everything in this book is for everyone.

I am a:	*I should:*
High School Student	Start with Chapter 1 or 2. Then read 3, 4, and 5. The goal is to skip 6 completely and go on to 7, 8 , 9, and 10
Freshman/ Sophomore	Start with Chapter 2. Then read 3, 4, and 5. The goal is to skip 6 completely and go on to 7, 8 , 9, and 10
Junior	Start with Chapter 5. Then come back and read 2, 3, and 4. The goal is to skip 6 completely and go on to 7, 8 , 9, and 10
Senior/ Grad Student	If graduating within 9 months, start with Chapter 6, and briefly look at 4. Then read 2, 7, and 8. If just starting grad school, read 3. If not already in grad school, briefly look at 9.

Chapter 1: College Selection

Key Concept:

Choose your college wisely. Don't assume you will keep your major and plan accordingly

You are a rare anomaly if you are a high school student reading this chapter in that you are incredibly ahead of the eight ball. If you aren't a high school student, skip ahead to the next chapter or refer to Chapter 0 for where you should be reading.

My father was a college recruiter for many years and his preferred group to work with was middle school students, because they hadn't made high school mistakes yet and there was more opportunity to structure their high school pathway to appeal to top colleges. Similarly, a high school student looking at colleges has more opportunities than a senior with nine months left before they have to deal with the real world.

You need to both think about the college and its accounting program when selecting a college. Otherwise you may end up in a college or program that isn't a good fit. Many good colleges have bad accounting programs or vice versa.

Similarly, you also should keep in mind that many people decide to change majors. I was one of them, because I was originally a business major and switched into accounting because I liked the classes and the promise of job security.

Let's start with the college. This book isn't about how to get into college, but I do want to give you some pointers of things to look at as you narrow down your list.

You should ask yourself the following *as you select a college*:

1. How will this college help me in the long run?
2. How will this college support my growth and be consistent with my values?
3. How much debt will I be taking on to go there?

The first of these questions looks at the big picture. What are the school's rankings? What are they known for? What do their students go on to do in life? What is their reputation? You can get a good education at a party school, but you may get the same or a better education at a "commuter school" or a conservative faith based school and not have to worry about the school's image when looking for a job. Above all, think about where you want to be in five, ten, and twenty years and whether the college is congruent with that goal.

The second of these questions is all about congruence with who you are as a person, and is critically important if you will be away from home and living at college. If you have causes or a faith background you are passionate about, make sure that the school has organizations that are consistent with your passions and will help you grow as a person. You will want to be very careful about choosing a school that is incongruent with your faith or passions, because it probably won't be the best choice. College is already stressful, and the last thing you need is an early midlife crisis brought on by haters. Many people pick colleges and then discover they hate the culture and spend a small fortune and lose precious time transferring someplace more to their liking.

The third and final question I would look at in choosing a college has to do with debt. Pay attention to the amount of debt you will have to take on to go to a college because it can come back to haunt you after you graduate and have to pay it off. It may make more sense to go to the commuter school down the street and live at home or take a full ride to a liberal arts college in the Northeast rather than moving to an unfamiliar area and attending a name brand college and incurring a lot of debt.

Now that we've discussed selecting a college, let's look at the accounting program. Here are some of the questions you want to ask yourself as you select an accounting program:

1. How well regarded and supported is this program?
2. How will I be able to distinguish myself in this program?
3. How many firms actively recruit from this program?
4. How hard is the transition process to another major and how well regarded are those majors?

The first of these questions gets to the meat of whether the college has a decent accounting program because it does you no good to join an accounting program that won't benefit you in the long run. I would start by researching whether the accounting program is AACSB or ACBSP accredited. If the college has one of these two accreditations, they clearly have a serious accounting program. Similarly, you want to look at the number of full time accounting faculty that the school has. If it's two or fewer, that's a major cause for concern. If it's less than five but they are accredited, then it is probably a smaller program overall which isn't necessarily bad or good. Finally, I would look at a random sample of partners and managers at accounting firms near the school. If you don't see alumni there, that's a cause for concern. If an unaccredited accounting program has a cause for concern, then I would avoid it. I would also avoid an accredited accounting program with two or fewer full time faculty members that doesn't have a decent alumni base.

Next, you want to look at what opportunities there are to distinguish yourself as part of the program. You want to be able to stand out and explore your interests within the discipline. Smaller programs should still have some opportunities or should have opportunities in conjunction with other business related programs. A lack of opportunities indicates a program that is an afterthought, not a serious contender. If you can't stand out, you probably should pick another college.

You also want to look at recruitment. Fewer firms will directly recruit from smaller programs because it doesn't make economic sense to do so. Larger programs should have a robust recruiting process in place with a variety of firms. This means that if you end up like me and don't do spectacularly in a smaller program, you will have to hustle to find a job where you might have an easier go of it in a larger program.

Finally, you need to think about the possibility that you will change majors. Some colleges don't let you switch schools and some don't let you switch majors. If you can switch majors, sometimes you run into issues because the general education requirements are different between majors and schools. This can create a real headache and it's better to prepare for it now than waiting until you are in the thick of things. Similarly, it does you no good to go to a college that has a great accounting program but mediocre alternative programs. You will spending far too much of your precious time and money to end up with a degree that isn't worth the paper it's printed on. If you are between two schools and the only difference is that one would be difficult to switch majors or that other majors aren't particularly good, pick the one that is less difficult or has better alternative majors.

I know that some people may have other things they look at in looking at colleges, but this is my quick and simple list of factors to look at that is based on my experiences both before and during colleges. One of the jokes I will often make to staff is that it would be interesting to see where I would have ended up had I gone to the far cheaper commuter school with a massive alumni base and a robust accounting program near the expensive private school that had a smaller accounting program that I ended up going to instead.

Since this is the only place in this book where I talk about college selection, I wish you the best of luck before we move on from it completely to setting up your board, a topic I strongly recommend you read regardless of what major you end up in.

Let's Review:

- ✓ You want to make sure you understand what you are getting yourself into when choosing a college because transferring can be expensive and a waste of resources.
- ✓ Look at both the college and the accounting program when making your decision.
- ✓ Understand the amount of debt you'll take on to attend the college and program.
- ✓ Make sure you understand the process for selecting alternative majors and any pitfalls or issues from doing so.

Chapter 2: Setting up your board

Key Concept:

You want to establish a board of advisors as soon as possible to guide your career.

You may have heard before that you should have a board of directors for your career, which is one of the things I didn't do that I regret the most. I call it a board of advisors, not directors, because ultimately you should be making life decisions.

However, having a group of advisors or mentors is great in any profession because it may set you up for an interview down the road but it also will help you navigate some potential pitfalls.

The key with these people is to spark and nurture an authentic relationship with them. Keep them informed of your successes and failures and involve them in critical decisions where they can provide useful input and then make sure to thank them and let them know what happened.

People naturally like to be helpful, and if people don't know what you are doing, they can't help you get there.

I won't tell you exactly who should be on your board of advisors, but I will give you some advice. If I were to go back and set up a board of advisors, I would want about five to eleven people, with the group as a whole having the following characteristics:

- ✓ At least one to three recent graduates of your accounting program who did well and are employed for big to medium sized firms
- ✓ At least two to five senior managers and partners at big and medium sized firms
- ✓ At least one or two accountants who now run their own firms having between 10 and 20 years of experience
- ✓ At least one or two accounting faculty members you get along with and have relevant experience

The first category of advisors will be most helpful as you navigate the accounting program and the many opportunities for involvement offered to you. They may also give you pointers or insights on events to attend or put in a good word for you when you apply to their firm.

The second category of advisors will be helpful in general in giving you a higher level understanding of practical accounting and firm dynamics. They also may be able to positively influence things for you when you apply to their firm, but you shouldn't expect this and should utilize them to direct your career.

The third category of advisors is one that I've added based on my own experiences. A lot of accountants end up out on their own. These advisors may be able to give you a higher level understanding of practical accounting, but they may also be useful in finding opportunities that aren't as well known and once you start your practice will be invaluable in navigating the unfamiliar waters of business ownership.

The fourth category is especially important if you plan or think you might go on to grad school. Even if you hate the idea of going to grad school, it is a great idea to have accounting faculty as mentors because they can help you navigate the program and they may know alumni willing to help you. Accounting faculty with non-academic experience may be able to provide you with additional insight on life after college.

Your biggest question now is probably how you would find these people.

I would approach each category differently, focusing on the middle two categories first. You want to fill these two categories as soon as possible and then come back and fill the other two. If you're about to graduate, then the first category may be more useful for help in navigating life after college.

Your first stop should be whatever your school calls career services. Even if you aren't in school yet, feel free to reach out to them, or go through admissions to get to them. They should be able to provide you with information on alumni that satisfy the first three categories.

The second stop should be the Internet. Even if career services gives you a lot of names, use the Internet to find more. Look for some connection, then try to set up an informational interview with them. The key is to have great questions and not waste their time, something I discuss in depth in the next chapter.

The third stop should be professors. If you don't know any right now, reach out to them and let them know that you are looking for mentors and they may know alumni for you to talk to.

The most important thing here is to be fearless, especially if you use informational interviewing to find mentors. As long as you are respectful and don't waste their time, you should be able to connect with people and convert them into mentors.

The other important thing, as I've mentioned before, is to stay connected with these people. Send Thanksgiving cards with a quick note and brief thank you emails at major milestones or when you make a decision based on their feedback. This will reinforce the connection and may lead to you getting a great opportunity further on that you wouldn't have otherwise gotten. It will also be helpful later on in your career, as I will discuss in a later chapter.

Let's Review:

- ✓ You want to establish a board of advisors as soon as possible to guide your career.
- ✓ This board should have specific types of individuals who will provide different expertise
- ✓ Don't be afraid to reach out to people who might make great mentors simply because of who they are.
- ✓ You need to remain connected with the advisors and make them feel engaged to get the most benefit from them

Chapter 3: Informational interviewing

Key Concept:

Informational interviewing is an underutilized but valuable tool to locate board members and potential internship or career opportunities.

You've probably heard of the concept of informational interviewing before, but very few people actually do it. I honestly regret not doing this in college, because it would have opened some doors for me when looking for a job and may have made the process much easier.

The basic idea behind informational interviewing is to establish connections in a field. It plays on the basic human desire to be seen as helpful to cultivate a relationship that can later be incredibly useful for career advancement.

If you play your cards right, not only will you acquire valuable intelligence about the field, but people will tell you exactly what they are looking for when they hire staff. This gives you an incredible advantage over other applicants because you can better tailor your application to what they are looking for.

The beauty of it is that it can be used for any field you might be interested in and can be done earlier than college. In fact, I strongly believe that it is most effective when done well before college.

Here is the basic process for how to do informational interviewing:

1. Make a list of firms you might want to work at and work with career services and professors to get introductions or Google and LinkedIn to find school alumni.
2. Reach out to partners and directors via email. Try not to do this during busy seasons if possible. This email needs to do the following three things
   a. State how you are connected to them
   b. Express interest in their field
   c. Provide some brief background information
   d. Ask for about 15 minutes by phone or over coffee to ask them questions about their field and what they think makes for an effective accountant.
3. Maximize the time they give you and ask really good questions, listen to the flow of the conversation, and let them do most of the talking. You want them to remember you in a good way.
4. Thank them for their time and stay in touch. If you develop a good connection, consider turning them into an advisor.

I cannot stress the importance of the initial contact, great questions, and the follow up enough. The initial contact is your first and possibly only chance to make a positive impression. Even if they don't chat with you, you will likely be applying to their firm later on and you want them to remember you as the person who was motivated enough to reach out for advice.

Similarly, great questions are important because you don't want to waste their time. The key here is to make a positive impression and be memorable as being brilliant. I don't want you to get too caught up in what is or isn't a great question, so I'll briefly give you what I would look at. My rule for a great question is twofold:

1. It can't be answered by a Google search
2. It asks for relevant opinion or follows up on research that the partner or director is familiar with.

I'm intentionally not providing examples of great questions because authenticity is key and unfortunately people have a nasty habit of copying and pasting things, which devalues their use. One thing to keep in mind, which I personally hate, is that any question you could have answered yourself or researched the answer to is a bad question. I don't mind being asked for my opinion, but I'd expect the person to have done at least some research on the subject area. The best example I can give of this is that if you were to reach out to Warren Buffett or the national chairman of a Big 4 accounting firm, you would want to ask them about their opinion on something based on your research that they could answer, not something basic or trivial.

I do have one caveat about research or trends. You need to keep your audience in mind and what their confirmable interests are. You only want to ask opinions on things they would have a reason to know and care about. Thus, questions about what makes a great staff member, specific aspects of their firm's culture, and things they wish they knew graduating college are always good but asking a partner in a specific industry questions about another industry or things that don't plausibly relate to your future as an accountant is a bad idea.

I also want to stress the importance of thanking the person and leaving the door open to follow-up. You may not think common courtesy is valuable, but it is and leads to a positive impression of you. The last thing you want is to apply for a job later and have your application killed because you were rude or ungrateful for the precious time that someone gave you out of their incredibly busy day.

Follow-up is critical as well. You had to work to get this connection, so it's in your best interests to maximize the value you get from it. I'm not saying you need to send out a monthly newsletter, but if you use information they gave you and it helps you, send them a brief note to let them know. Similarly, if you later have follow-up questions, use these as an opportunity to for additional contact.

There is no single right way to do informational interviewing, but there are some wrong ways. The most important thing about it is just to do it because it will make your life slightly easier down the road.

Let's Review:

- ✓ Informational interviewing allows you to get connections and information about a specific career path.
- ✓ You need to maximize any time given and remember you are dealing with busy professionals.
- ✓ Don't be stupid or do stupid things.
- ✓ Always exercise common courtesy and follow-up.

Chapter 4: Networking

Key Concept:

Humans are social animals. Knowing the right person can launch your career.

Some of you will love this chapter. Others will be like me and hate it because of the subject matter.

I have a love-hate relationship with networking. I love to hate it but begrudgingly accept it as a necessary evil. My hatred of it is probably why I didn't do more of it in college. Yet, now I have to network as a business owner to both find clients and maintain my reputation within the field.

I want to make it clear that this is not a chapter on how to network but a chapter on the importance of networking. Far too much ink has been spilled on how to network by your career services office and the Internet.

I've previously mentioned that many of the "best jobs" in accounting are reserved for those who have good grades and interview well. However, if you don't fit these criteria then networking may give you a second chance.

Even if you do meet these criteria, networking can also get you people to run informational interviews with or potential advisors for your board. As painful as it is to say, networking can only help you out. So where should you network?

The first place you should look at is opportunities your school offers you. You would be surprised how many people don't bother to show up for opportunities. This is their loss because usually food is involved and sometimes other benefits. As an example, I once got an initial interview just because I showed up to a random firm's presentation on campus and got another interview because I spoke with a recruiter at a career fair. You can't win a race you don't show up to compete in.

If you go to career fairs or meet the firms, I always recommend going in reverse order of prestige. Start with the smaller and less popular firms first. You will be able to warm up and you'll make more effective use of your time than waiting in line. Don't worry about being memorable as much as making a connection and getting a card. Jot one or two quick notes on the back of each card and send them a thank you email after the fact that references how they were helpful. Focus on finding out what they are looking for in applicants and information about their firm's culture.

You also want to participate in any alumni-student relations programs your school offers. These programs give you the opportunity to meet influential alumni and grow your network for a minimal time commitment.

Second, you need to expand your horizons and get creative. There is a lot of competition for jobs among your fellow students, so you want to get a slight advantage on them.

One excellent way to do this is to get involved in local service and social groups that have influential members. These are untapped opportunities to make real connections that will benefit you both in finding a job and later if you decide to open a practice.

The other way to do this is professional associations. In particular, you should look at participating in local CPA society chapters or local enrolled agent society chapters. Many will run a monthly dinner meeting where you'll be able to meet practicing professionals and firm owners. These can be slightly pricey, but it is worth the opportunity to meet people who may be able to help move your career forward especially since other students likely won't be there to compete for attention. Your focus here has be on developing real relationships with people and learning, not hunting for work, or otherwise you'll just annoy people.

The most important thing about any networking you do is to remember that first impressions do matter and that the fortune is in the follow-up. Similar to informational interviewing, you've invested time in connecting with people and it's in your best interests to maximize the value from these connections. You want to briefly follow up with new connections to thank them for their time, referencing something they said or did that was valuable to you.

If it makes sense, continue the conversation from there and potentially turn them into a mentor. Even if you don't continue the conversation, keep track of every person you've connected with and remember the importance of common courtesy. You never know where people will end up and how they will be in position to help or hinder you. As the saying goes, "Be nice to those you meet on the way up, because they will be there on the way down and they may have baseball bats to express their appreciation for your discourtesy".

Let's Review:

- ✓ Think outside the box when networking
- ✓ Take full advantage of on campus opportunities
- ✓ Connect with local CPA and EA groups to expand your network
- ✓ Remember the importance of follow-up and common courtesy

Chapter 5: Internships/Seasonal work

> **Key Concept**:
>
> Internships and seasonal work can turn into a career or provide relevant experience to improve your prospects of finding a great job

Internships and seasonal work are an undervalued aspect of accounting. I personally think they are easier to get than full time permanent positions, they may help you qualify for licensure faster, and they help boost your resume. What's not to like?

The only downside of internships and seasonal work is when employers don't grasp that you are a student first and aren't flexible with scheduling.

There are two types of recruiting processes you need to keep in mind. These are:

1. How the Big 4 and mid-tier firms find and hire entry level staff
2. How everybody else finds and hires staff

This chapter will primarily discuss the second category with a heavy emphasis on internships and seasonal work at small to medium sized firms. I will briefly chat about the internship process at Big 4 and mid-tier firms, but I want to make sure you understand all the opportunities available to you since some accounting programs can lull you into a false sense of security before your senior year or obsessively focus only on the first category when the second is far more advantageous for most students.

How the Big 4 and Mid-Tier Firms Recruit

Let's start by discussing the Big 4 and mid-tier recruiting process. These firms have a systematic recruiting process that focuses on filling entry level positions well in advance of their needs.

The first step in many larger firms' recruiting processes are summer conferences targeted toward rising sophomores and juniors. These are experiences that are between one and two weeks in length.

The next step, which many colleges emphasize heavily, is the summer internship process. Firms are targeting current juniors for internships between their junior and senior year. These are eight to ten week experiences that allow for firms to evaluate students in the firm environment. 90% of these internships turn into full time offers following graduation. The problem with waiting to apply to these internships is that it wastes two years of your college career when you could have been interning with a small firm.

The final step, which is much more competitive and harder to get hired through is entry level hiring. There are much fewer positions available that all the accounting students who didn't get an internship or are desperate to find a job are competing for. The firms already filled most of their positions through their internship program and can afford to be highly selective. Further, if the firm filled all their spots through the internship program, which has happened, they won't be hiring any additional entry level staff.

Even if the firm doesn't have an internship program, they will still be able to fill all their available positions relatively quickly for the reasons I mentioned.

The major problem with focusing on this recruiting process is that there are relatively few positions available, which decrease the closer you get to graduate and are primarily reserved for the students with decent grades and interview skills.

How Everybody Else Recruits

The problem with getting sucked into how the larger firms recruit is that you can potentially overlook a multitude of great jobs that are either not advertised or very lightly advertised.

Here are some general premises that underlie how everyone else (including me) who isn't a large firm recruits:

1. We hate recruiting and hiring with a passion
2. We initiate the recruiting process only when absolutely unavoidable
3. We are busy and may have enough work for an intern but haven't thought about it.

The key thing to understand here is that recruiting is a real pain. I only get paid when my staff or I do client service work, not reading resumes or conducting interviews. Even worse, I may have to pay to advertise the job and get 20 mediocre applications from unqualified applicants. It's the same scenario for almost any accounting or tax business owner. Some of us solve this issue by working with recruiters to fill openings, but many of us just don't bother to waste our time and put recruiting off.

We may not actively recruit, but that doesn't mean we don't have staffing needs. It's just that the hiring process is so painful that it's delayed until absolutely necessary. This doesn't mean that we settle for mediocre candidates out of desperation, but it means that we are incredibly incentivized to hire the right candidate.

We also may not have thought about bringing in an intern or seasonal associate. Many of us are so busy that we're only focused on what's in front of us, not one month or one year down the line. As a result, you may end up with an internship or seasonal work just because your resume arrived at the right time when we are experiencing an influx of work.

Finally, there are many more of us than there are big 4 or mid-tier firms and we may have more opportunities to gain diverse skills and direct mentorship than a more regimented larger firm where you may only work on a narrow project and rarely see the engagement partner.

Each of these premises is why you should consider applying outside the larger firms and do so well before your junior year if possible. You might not have much accounting background, but you still might be able to find an internship or position. Even if you just are doing clerical work, it will give you exposure to how accounting works and functions.

Before I talk about how to effectively and systematically apply to small firms, let's quickly address interviewing since you may have questions about it. There is a lot of ink spilled on the topic and many wonderful resources on how interview, so I won't spend long on the topic, but it is relatively important. A lot of otherwise qualified candidates, including yours truly, just don't interview well.

The most important thing to remember about interviewing is to let the interviewer talk, exercise common courtesy at all times, and assume everyone you meet is part of the interview. It may seem counter intuitive, but there is some research to show that interviewers consider interviews more positively when they do most of the speaking. Finally, you need to have about eight good questions for the interviewer if they ask if you have questions. See Chapter 2 for my philosophy on questions.

Interviewing ability is important, but the key here when applying to smaller firms is that you have to be incredibly systematic and fully leverage your local area and network.

Here's a sample process I would use to find internships and seasonal work.

1. Open an Excel file and create a spreadsheet with the following columns:
   a. Firm Name
   b. Connection?
   c. Demographic
   d. Partner/HR Name
   e. Email Address
   f. Date Applied
   g. Date Response

     h.   Interview Date

     i.   Offer?

2. Go through your list of contacts and add anyone you or family or close friends know who is an accountant or to the excel file. Put "personal" for connection.

3. Reach out to career services and see if any firms occasionally hire interns or have historically hired interns and get a list of local alumni who are accountants. Put "school" for connection.

4. Pull up the top 100 accounting firms and find all the firms with at least one office in your area and add them to the excel file.

5. Search for accounting and tax firms in your local area as well as major companies with accounting departments on Google in your area and add them to the excel file. You may need to search multiple times to find every firm.

6. Research every single one of the firms on your excel file and review the staff bios. If the staff worked at another firm, check to see if it is still in business and add it to the excel file and repeat the staff bio search process with that firm. Put "school" under connection for any firm with a contact that is an alumni and "n/a" for everything else.

7. Research each firm and put EP under demographic if they have an existing formal recruitment process. If the firm doesn't have a formal process, then put 1P for firms with one licensed professional and MP for firms with more than one licensed professional. If a firm has multiple professionals and offices, put MO under demographic.

8. Research each non EP firm listed as n/a for the managing partner's information. If they have multiple offices, find either the partner who runs the group you want to work in or the office you

want to work in. If this person is an alumni, update the connection field to "school"

9. Sort your list as follows:
   a. First, by demographic
   b. Second, by connection
10. Draft a basic cover letter and resume inquiring about internship or seasonal opportunities that can be tailored to each firm. Make sure to specify when you are looking to start and end work and the maximum number of hours you are available to work. Don't say "N hours", say "up to N hours". See Appendix B for tips.
11. Apply to the EP firms through their recruiting process or through your connection there if you have one. If you can't apply through a connection, make sure your connection is aware you are applying. Keep an eye on their deadlines.
12. Systematically customize and send your resume with a cover email or your resume and a cover letter to each firm on the list when they are likely to be considering employees. You'll want to work with your mentors to figure out when this is. Start with MO, then MP, then 1P. You can also ask that they send your resume on to colleagues who may be hiring.
13. Track all responses. If you get any responses back from smaller firms or managing partners that they aren't hiring, send a quick thank you and ask if they know any colleagues who might be hiring. If you haven't already applied to the colleague, repeat steps 6 through 10 for them.
14. Book interviews promptly but make sure to call firms you are most interested in working for first and book them first. Always send thank you cards to the hiring manager, the interviewer, and the receptionist if you go to their office. If you aren't

given an offer, feel free to ask how you can improve your skills to become more competitive.

15. When you receive an offer, make sure you understand the terms of the offer and when they need a response. You may be expected to accept on the spot, which is why you want to book more preferred firms first. Do your research on what market compensation is in your area before your interview. If you are applying to an EP, MO, or MP firm, compensation information may be available on Glass Door. Otherwise, look at local hiring ads for accounting firms that state an hourly rate. Follow up on non-responsive interviews about one week after the interview.

This may seem daunting, but by following this or a similar process, you will be able to effectively and efficiently apply to the firms that are most likely to be able to offer you a short term opportunity.

Now that you hopefully have some short term opportunities to consider, I want to talk about some pitfalls you need to watch out for. The most common ones are bait and switch and misclassification as contract labor.

A bait and switch is any scenario where one thing is offered or promised and then swapped for something else later. An example of this I experienced was when I applied for a salaried retirement plans specialist position with a major financial services company (I was really desperate to find a job!) but when I showed up to interview, I found out I was being interviewed for a commission based financial advisor position. The concerning thing here is that this was a listing posted through my school's job board and was presumably vetted.

This most commonly happens before or at the interview, but can also happen even after the interview where the type of work or compensation suddenly changes. It is particularly common on Craigslist, which is why I don't recommend applying to job postings there.

The other pitfall is misclassification as contract labor. Employees can be expensive between payroll taxes and workers compensation laws. Employers are incentivized to reduce costs and some will cut corners by offering to "1099" people who should be employees. This means that the employer does no tax withholding, which can set the employee up for a massive tax bill and potential consequences from local authorities for not having a business license. Independent contractors are also not covered under workers compensation, unemployment or state disability insurance, which means if you get hurt or are terminated unfairly, you're on your own.

I use both interns and independent contractors. Here are the core differences between them.

Interns and employees usually:

- ✓ Are subject to the employer's supervision and control about when, where and how to work
- ✓ Don't have unreimbursed business expenses
- ✓ Are restricted in their ability to accept work from external sources
- ✓ Are guaranteed a regular wage amount for a specified period of time

An example of an employee is an intern who does data entry for a CPA during tax season in his office with a computer and software provided by the CPA and is paid an hourly rate for their work and works a set schedule. The intern is clearly an employee because they work under the supervision of the CPA and have little discretion over when, where and how to work. Further, the intern has a set schedule and is paid for hours worked regardless of work performed, which eliminates the risk usually seen in business.

Independent contractors usually

- ✓ Choose when, where and how to work
- ✓ Have unreimbursed business expenses
- ✓ Are unrestricted in their ability to accept work from external sources and are free to accept or reject specific projects
- ✓ Are paid per project or milestone

An example of an independent contractor is a licensed tax preparer who prepares tax returns remotely for a CPA using their own computer and software and is paid per completed return and retains the ability to accept or reject work. The preparer is clearly an independent contractor because they work independently and exercise discretion over where, when, and how to work. Further, the preparer only gets paid when they complete tax returns, which means that the preparer has risk.

The important thing here is to make sure to read any agreement you are provided and that you understand how you are being paid and the firm's expectations of you. If you are being expected to pay for a license or expenses before you are able to be paid, make sure that it is realistic for you to get some return on this investment before you agree to an agreement. If the contract looks particularly unusual, have a mentor or your career services office look at it with you.

Let's Review:

- ✓ Most colleges and students focus too much on large firms and miss out on opportunities at smaller firms
- ✓ Smaller firms may be able to provide more interaction with partners and better mentorship opportunities
- ✓ You need to utilize an effective and systematic process to identify and apply to potential employers that leverages your personal and college network.
- ✓ Never assume a firm is too small to need help
- ✓ Beware of Craigslist and watch out for bait and switch tactics and work arrangements that aren't in your best interest.

Chapter 6: Finding a Job in a Rush

> **Key Concept**:
>
> It is hard, but still possible to find a great job in a rush. This is a numbers game and hustle is essential.

I suspect that many of you who are reading this book are seniors who have about nine months left before you have to deal with the cruel reality of life after college and don't have a job lined up. No, I'm not psychic. I just was in your shoes once staring at my graduation date from Pepperdine and seriously contemplating whether a fast food uniform was in my future.

The good news is that it's entirely possible to find a job, even in the eleventh hour. The bad news is that it requires a lot of work if you haven't already done at least some of the things I discussed in Chapters 2 through 5. The only thing I had going for me starting my senior year is that I was starting an internship, but I still managed to find a great job that set me up for success.

Here's the step by step approach I took:

1. Open an Excel file and create a spreadsheet with the following columns:
   a. Firm Name
   b. Hiring Manager Name, Position

    c. Email
    d. Position Applied For
    e. Date Applied
    f. Date Response
    g. Interview Date
    h. Offer?

2. Pull up the top 100 accounting firms and find all the firms with at least one office in your area and add them to the excel file

3. Search for accounting and tax firms as well as major companies with accounting departments on Google in your area and add them to the excel file.

4. Research every single one of the firms on your excel file and review the staff bios. If the staff worked at another firm, check to see if it is still in business and add it to the excel file and repeat the staff bio search process with that firm.

5. Research each firm and try to locate a hiring manager name and email or the managing partner's name and email. Also connect with your college's career services office to help you find info or if they recruit on campus. If you can't find one, then you'll use mail instead.

6. Draft a basic cover letter and resume that can be tailored to each firm. See Appendix B for tips.

7. Systematically customize and send your resume with a cover email or your resume and a cover letter to each firm on the list. You want to specifically inquire about seasonal or full time opportunities with their firm when you do this. You can also ask that they send your resume on to colleagues who may be hiring.

8. Track all responses. If you get any responses back from smaller firms or managing partners that they aren't hiring, send a quick thank you and ask if they know any colleagues who might be hiring. If you

haven't already applied to the colleague, repeat steps 4 through 7 for them.

9. Book interviews promptly and always send thank you cards to the hiring manager, the interviewer, and the receptionist if you go to their office. If you aren't given an offer, feel free to ask how you can improve your interview skills. See Chapter 5 for more on interviewing.
10. When you receive an offer, make sure you understand the terms of the offer and when they need a response.

I could go through each step in gory detail, but I will spare you because it won't help you. Instead, I'll briefly discuss what to do about out of town firms, Craigslist, temp agencies, and recruiters before I walk through my results.

First, let's talk about out of town firms and what your area is. I get questions sometimes about how far your area extends and whether to apply to firms that are out of town. Your area is the geographic area where you live, plus the sphere of influence of your college. A firm is out of town if it is not within your area. The only out of town employer I applied to was a state agency. I usually don't recommend applying out of town to private employers unless you have ties to the area or can articulate a reason for wanting to live or work there. Otherwise, the firm may not take you seriously as a candidate.

Second, let's talk about Craigslist. I didn't really apply to any listings on Craigslist nor do I hire on Craigslist because most of the listings where I live are either junk or disguised "business opportunities". I would treat all Craigslist postings with caution for this reason.

Third, let's talk about temp agencies. There are several agencies that will find you accounting jobs. The problem is that they won't pay very well. It's a great way to get experience if you're desperate, but you will need to fight for the pay you deserve.

The same applies with recruiters. They can either be really good or really bad. One of the worst interviews I had was set up by a recruiter, who clearly didn't realize I wasn't qualified for the job and was just trying to meet a quota. Make sure to research recruiters and the firms they represent and proceed with caution when applying through them. You will also want to watch out for financial services recruiters who will trick you into thinking you are applying for a job when you are applying for a business opportunity. Always do your research on the recruiter and the company and beware recruiters who absolutely refuse to tell you who the company is or are evasive. Also beware of recruiters who call you out of the blue or reference an application not on your list of firms.

The key thing to remember with all this is that is a numbers game. The point of the extensive research finding firms is to find as many firms as possible to apply to in order to increase interviews and potential offers. In my case, I sent out 200 resumes, which yielded:

- ✓ 15-20 phone interviews (~8-10%)
- ✓ 5 in person interviews (1 in 3 phone interviews)
- ✓ 2 offers (40%)

I also received an interview invitation as I was starting my job and recommended another accounting student to them I knew was looking for work.

This basically is the best process I know to find work in a rush but before I move on to life after college, I want to address the numbers quickly. There is no magic number for how many applications you need to send out to find a job. If I were desperate, lacked meaningful connections or experience, and looking for work, I would send out a resume to almost anyone I think is hiring. However, you also might be able to send out a smaller or larger number of resumes and achieve the same results by using qualifiers or disqualifiers.

Qualifiers and disqualifiers are a concept from sales used to focus resources on leads and prospects that are more likely to be closed ("turned into sales"). For example, time share companies look for people who are 28 years or older and make $75,000 per year because their internal research shows that these people are more likely to be able and willing to buy a timeshare.

The upside of qualifiers is that it can both decrease the number of contacts needed to achieve a desired result and increase the success rate associated with those contacts. The downside, in searching for accounting jobs, is that it can be hard to design and implement qualifiers because most accounting firm websites are garbage and don't allow you to accurately assess the firm's size.

Further, qualifiers wouldn't account for the fact that some firms have unexpected openings or staff needs. For these reasons, while it is smart to send out resumes in order of firm size, I would recommend sending resumes to anyone who might be hiring rather than trying to qualify your list too much or assuming a firm is too small.

Let's Review:

- ✓ Locating a job in a rush is a numbers game
- ✓ You need to systemically and efficiently send out your resume to as many potential employers as possible.
- ✓ Never assume a firm is too small to need help
- ✓ Be cautious with Craigslist, recruiters, and temp agencies to avoid getting ripped off or pushed into a bad situation

Chapter 7: Life Out of College

Key Concept:

Decisions you make now will affect the rest of your career

This chapter is one of the more unique ones in this book because it talks about a topic that colleges never talk about but really should. I want to spend a little time chatting about life out of college and some of the stupid mistakes you can make that will screw up your future and prevent you from reaching financial invincibility.

Financial invincibility, also referred to as financial freedom, is the point at which you are immune from financial loss from everything except your own stupidity or total economic collapse. This means that you don't care what happens in life, because you are financially secure. You may not think this is important now, but imagine facing a crisis and the peace of not having to worry about money. Consequently, financial invincibility is one of the most powerful things in the world and something you should strive for, especially since you will have the income coming in to make it a reality if you manage your money properly.

The important thing to keep in mind is that money is neither good nor bad. Money does it what it is told. If you are prudent and use money wisely, then it will be your friend. If you don't, then it will crush you under the weight of poor decisions.

I recommend you follow some basic concepts when you get out of college to get to financial invincibility:

1. Live below your means
2. Get rid of all consumer debt as soon as possible
3. Establish a robust emergency fund
4. Systematically eliminate any student loans
5. Diversify and protect your income
6. Become an owner, not a renter

Live below your means

Let's start with the most important of these, living below your means. One of the biggest mistakes most people make is that they increase their consumption as their income increases rather than living below their means and saving or investing the difference. Similarly, as you get bonuses and raises, use a small part of that money to reward yourself with something nice and then save or invest the difference.

The key thing here is that you don't need to keep up with the Joneses. Instead, you should get a head start on making yourself financially invincible.

Get rid of all consumer debt as soon as possible

The first step on the road to financial invincibility is establishing a starter emergency fund of $500 to $1,000 and then immediately eliminating all consumer debt.

The key thing to understand about debt is that when you are in debt to someone, you are literally their slave. They own your life and the fruits of your labor, not you. You must pay them each month or they will take your stuff or "ruin your credit".

All debt is problematic, but consumer debt is particularly dangerous because you are borrowing money at a high rate of interest from other people and it is easy to get in over your head through impulse purchases. If you end up with $10,000 in credit card debt at 24% interest, you will be paying at least $200 per month in interest only, when you could be investing that money and making between $2 to $20 per month in passive income instead.

You want to be strategic in eliminating your consumer debt. You may want to look at consolidating your debts into one lower interest loan. The key is that you only want to consolidate the debts that have higher interest rates than the loan you are replacing them with.

Once you are finishing consolidating debts, there are two general ways to pay them off. One way is to pay off debts from smallest to largest balance due. This is great if you need small victories to remain engaged because it will reinforce your decision and make you feel the impact of your decision. The other way, which is better if you don't need small victories to stick to a long term plan, is to pay off the highest interest debts first because you will pay less overall. Either way, you want to immediately stop using consumer debt and have a systematic approach to paying it off.

Establish a robust emergency fund

The next step on the road to financial invincibility is to establish a robust emergency fund. This is a more extensive version of the starter emergency fund. You will want to look into a high yield savings account to keep your emergency fund in, preferably one that is at a different bank than your checking account to avoid the temptation to raid it for impulse purchases. You never want to invest your emergency fund in anything other than cash, or use it for non-essential or impulse purchases. Your goal is to consistently put away money to get to the point where you have at least 6 months of expenses in the savings account. Once you reach this point, you will want to divert your monthly savings into investments.

The idea with the emergency fund is to provide you with breathing room in an emergency. Otherwise you would likely max out your credit cards to solve the problem, creating more consumer debt and perpetuating a vicious cycle of living paycheck to paycheck and being a slave to your creditors. If you ever have to use the emergency fund, you should immediately stop investing until you get back up to 6 months of expenses in the fund.

Systematically eliminate any student loans

Student loans are both a blessing and a curse. They allow greater access to higher education, but have also increased the overall cost of higher education and cripple many adults with monthly payments. You will want to systematically work to eliminate student loans unless you are participating in public interest loan forgiveness and are confident you will get to the 10 years of employment. Otherwise you will end up paying a small fortune in interest over your lifetime. The best way to handle this is similar to credit cards. Consider consolidating all high interest loans into a lower interest loan and then pay toward either the highest interest rate or the lowest balance first.

Diversify and protect your income

The most important part of becoming financially invincible is diversifying and protecting your income. Even before you pay off debt, you want to make sure you have an appropriate long term disability insurance policy. These are fairly inexpensive and will provide you with income replacement if you become disabled, which can be the difference between survival and homelessness. As an accountant, if you can't work and you don't have disability insurance, you won't be in good shape.

Next, you absolutely must begin to diversify your income. The point of diversification is to protect yourself against various risks. Long term disability insurance protects you against the risk of becoming disabled. The other major risk you want to protect against is your job or business. You want to grow your investments first by diversifying your investments so you won't lose your portfolio to fees or a single investment failing, and then to the point that you are no longer solely reliant on your job for income. This will take a little time, but will make you truly financially invincible because the only thing that can actually harm you will be your own stupidity or total economic collapse.

Become an owner, not a renter

The final thing you want to do is consider becoming an owner, not a renter. Housing tends to be one of the biggest expenses on a monthly budget. If you rent an apartment, then you will pay money to someone else each month for the right to live there. The next month, you have to pay again and the money is lost forever.

What if you took that money and paid it to yourself or had other people paying you? This isn't as crazy of an idea as it sounds like. If you own a duplex or triplex and live in one unit and the rent the others, then other people are paying your mortgage for you and you are able to divert this money into other investments or paying down the mortgage faster. Either way, it puts you closer to financial invincibility faster.

Let's Review:

- ✓ You want to use your income in a way that helps you in the long run after college
- ✓ Avoid making stupid decisions or following conventional wisdom
- ✓ Be wary of debt
- ✓ Strive to reach financial invincibility.

Chapter 8: Licensure

I personally think that licensure is one of the most critical parts of being an accountant. You may be able to get your first job without being licensed, but you really need to be licensed to open up opportunities and earn what you're worth.

I say this because it has been true for me in that I get opportunities for work now just because I am a CPA and I got a significant raise at the firm I was working at once I became a CPA.

The primary license in accounting is the CPA certificate or license. If you want to do tax and don't want to work for bigger firms, then the EA credential might make sense instead. I will briefly come back to this credential, but first I want address the CPA credential because it is more dominant and broadly relevant.

The most important thing about the CPA credential to know is the three components to becoming a CPA, which are:

1. Education
2. Examination
3. Experience.

I will cover each of these generally but you should look on the NASBA website to find the exact requirements for your state because they do vary and can change over time.

You don't want to use other sites to find information on the CPA because they may be out of date or trying to sell you something. NASBA is the best resource for CPA licensing information because they include summaries for all 50 states and links to each states specific requirements.

Education

Every state requires a bachelor's degree for licensure, and most states require 150 semester or 225 quarter hours. Some states have specific requirements as to where and what type of bachelor's degree qualifies while others simply have specific coursework requirements.

If you will meet your state's requirements, great! If not, then the reason for the deficiency should drive your plan to remediate it. Avoid going to grad school immediately after graduating unless you are planning on working in tax, you have a pretty mediocre GPA, or you need a qualifying degree. I discuss grad school more in depth in the next chapter including my philosophy on why or why not you might want to go there.

The best alternative for resolving a credit deficiency, if your state allows it, is to either take the courses through a college extension program or at a community college. This will be much more cost effective and beneficial than grad school and the associated debt.

Examination

Every state requires that candidates pass the Uniform CPA exam to become licensed. In the past, this exam was taken all at one time and only offered a few days a year, but now it is taken in four parts which are officially referred to as sections, one part as a time, and offered during 9 months of the year. The passing score on each part of this exam is 75% or more.

The current four parts of the exam and the courses they are roughly equivalent to are as follows.

Exam Part	Course Equivalents
AUD	Auditing/Advanced Auditing
BEC	Economics/Finance/Cost Accounting/Advanced Cost Accounting
FAR	Financial Accounting/Intermediate Accounting/Advanced Accounting
REG	Business Law/Ethics/Taxation

You register for the exam through either NASBA or your state board, who will issue you a document called a Notice to Schedule (NTS). This NTS lists the exams you are registered for and allows you to book your appointment through Prometric to sit the exams.

The most important thing here is to get the tests booked as soon as possible and pick testing times and sites that are conducive to your sanity. You want to take these exams as soon as possible after you graduate, so at least some of the concepts are still in your head.

If your firm provides you with study materials or courses, use the materials they provide. Otherwise, start by reviewing your college materials and then look into a course provider like Ninja, where the materials actually match up to the current exam format and are designed to get people to pass.

If you fail an exam section, immediately schedule a new testing in the next window. Your goal is to pass the exams as soon as possible so you can get licensed as soon as you meet the experience requirement.

Some states have a stand-alone ethics exam requirement in addition to the CPA exam. This exam you can wait on until right before you are ready to apply, because the scores can expire and it should not require much study to pass.

Experience

The final CPA requirement is experience. All states require that candidates have the equivalent of one year of full time experience. Most states require this experience to be supervised by a CPA and some states require the experience to be in an accounting firm. Half of the states will allow candidates to accrue experience part time.

The most optimal outcome here if your state recognizes part time work is for you to do internships and seasonal work to either partially or fully satisfy the experience requirement. It can take up to 6 months for your license application to be processed once it's complete. This means that you might not be licensed until 18 months or more after graduation if you wait to do your experience after you graduate. By contrast, if you can get some or all of your experience done in college, then you may be a licensed CPA a few months into your first year. Plus, many larger firms award bonuses or raises for becoming a CPA, which can be larger in the first year working than subsequent years.

Enrolled Agent

An alternative licensure to the CPA for people who want to do tax accounting is the Enrolled Agent credential. If you want to be a big 4 or mid-tier firm staff member, this credential won't really do much for you. However, if you are working for a smaller accounting firm that just does tax, or are running into issues with the CPA exam, or want to open your own tax practice, then this may be a good idea to pursue instead or in conjunction with the CPA.

The Enrolled Agent credential is administered by the Internal Revenue Service and bestows the unlimited right to represent taxpayers before the IRS. In 48 states, it also serves as a stand-alone credential for tax services.

There is an experience and examination track to obtain the credential. The experience track is only open to IRS employees in qualifying positions. The examination track is open to the general public.

The appealing thing about being an Enrolled Agent is that there is no education or experience requirement if you are applying by examination.

The examination is broken into three parts consisting of 100 multiple choice questions, which can be scheduled at Prometric during 10 months of the year. Part I covers individuals, Part II covers businesses, and Part III covers practice and procedure. The best exam review course for this credential is run by Gleim. The most optimal way to take the exams if you have a decent tax background is Part III, Part I, and Part II. If you don't have a decent tax background or are weak in business taxation, then take Part II, Part I, and Part III.

Part of my strategy in finding a job was to become an Enrolled Agent, which I completed in the summer before my senior year. It was helpful with the job I ended up getting in that I got a higher pay grade for being licensed and enjoyed more independence than unlicensed staff. It didn't really do much for me though in applying to accounting firms.

The key thing that is really helped my career was becoming a CPA. Not only did I get an unexpected raise, but most of the opportunities I get now are because I'm a CPA not because I'm an EA.

Let's Review:

- ✓ You need to become licensed as soon as possible to get the best pay and opportunities
- ✓ Be careful about going to grad school to satisfy credit deficiencies
- ✓ Get as much experience done as soon as possible so you can apply for licensure as soon as possible
- ✓ Consider becoming an Enrolled Agent if you want to do tax and your firm supports it

---

Chapter 9: Grad School

Key Concept:

Only go to graduate school if it fits into your long term goals and make sure the program you select will further those goals.

It's becoming incredibly more common for accounting students to go to grad school, which is concerning because it is actually unnecessary and counter-productive in some cases.

I remember when I graduated, my college didn't have a masters in accounting program, but the following year one was implemented. A similar theme was taking place at various other colleges in the area and across the United States due to full implementation of the 150 hour requirement.

At the same time, MBA programs, which had become a cash cow for colleges, were declining in popularity. I doubt the timing was a coincidence.

The two major decisions you will face when considering grad school are:

1. When and why should I go to grad school?
2. What school and program should I go to?

I want to talk about when people should go to grad school first and then the different programs that are available.

You can either go to grad school immediately after college or wait a few years and then go. You should only go to grad school immediately after college if any of the following apply:

- ✓ You are planning on working in tax
- ✓ You have a pretty mediocre GPA
- ✓ You need a qualifying degree to become a CPA

It's better in many cases to wait a few years and then think about going to grad school. This may be more advantageous because you will have work experience, will have reduced your undergraduate student loans, and will be a CPA which can work in your favor.

There are five types of grad school programs you may consider. These are:

- ✓ Doctoral accounting programs
- ✓ Law school
- ✓ Business school
- ✓ Graduate tax programs
- ✓ Graduate accounting programs.

Let's take each of these separately and discuss the merits and disadvantages of each.

Doctoral accounting programs

The first grad school program is the rarest one for accounting students to do, doctoral programs. The primary reason for going to a doctoral program is to teach accounting. I do not recommend going into a doctoral program right out of undergrad because it is better to become licensed and get work experience first.

The major advantage to this grad school program is that the vast majority of doctoral students are funded by the school. This means that the school pays you to attend, but they may expect you to have some teaching or research responsibilities.

The major disadvantage is that there are relatively few candidacies which can be intensely competitive. If you didn't do well academically in undergrad, you probably will find it difficult to go to an AACSB accredited doctoral program.

Your focus in the program will be on research skills and developing and defending an original scholarly work called a dissertation. Once you complete your dissertation and graduate, you will then likely apply for employment as a tenure track professor at various schools across the US. If this doesn't seem interesting, then this probably isn't the grad school program for you.

Law school

Another option for accounting students is law school. It is not uncommon for accounting students or accountants to get law degrees. Keep in mind that not everyone with a law degree becomes a lawyer. As with doctoral programs, I don't recommend going to law school straight out of college. You really want to get some work experience first.

Admissions starts by looking at your GPA and LSAT score. Other parts of your application only come into play once you pass the GPA and LSAT hurdle.

Law school is a three to four year exercise in learning how to think and approach problems analytically. You should not go to law school if you are weak at problem solving because you'll run into issues. Law school classes are graded on a curve, which tends to be harsher at lower ranked schools than higher ranked schools. This means that if you have difficulty with problem solving or didn't do well on the LSAT, law school will be very difficult for you and you probably won't do well.

In general, if you have a poor LSAT score, don't bother applying to law school because you'll be stuck with your choice of lower tier programs with harsh curves.

Some states allow unaccredited or state accredited law schools. You want to avoid these like the plague because you will be unable to practice in most states. Only consider ABA accredited law schools if you are planning on going to law school.

Business school

Another option for some accountants is business school (MBA). As with doctoral programs and law school, you don't want to do this right out of undergrad. The best programs require you to have some work experience before you apply.

The GMAT is one of the major factors in applying to business school. Some programs will waive the GMAT requirement if you are a CPA, but most programs will require it, even if it isn't looked at heavily. Admissions is usually based in part on undergraduate GPA and

GMAT score, but may take other factors into account depending on the school.

Business school focuses more on the skills necessary for operating businesses and managing people. A lot of the coursework is done in groups and grading tends to be more relaxed. Some business school programs will have prerequisites that aren't clear up front that have to be completed before you start the program and add additional costs. As with anything, you want to make sure you understand what you're getting into.

The downside of business school is that almost every college has an MBA program, and most aren't worth the paper they are printed on. Also, the sheer number of MBA degrees granted has somewhat diluted the value of the degree overall. You want to carefully evaluate any program you're considering and make sure it is AACSB accredited and look at the caliber of the faculty and their research focus and how it relates to your career plans.

Business school might make sense if you are dealing more with business consulting than accounting. If you are doing primarily accounting or tax work, then it probably won't make sense for you to pursue. Also, if you are looking for a qualifying degree, business school probably won't work for that purpose.

Graduate tax programs

The best grad school option for accountants working in tax is a graduate tax program. These degrees are usually labelled as masters in taxation (MT) or a master of science in taxation (MST). Some schools offer a masters of business taxation (MBT) which is functionally equivalent.

These programs are great because they will provide you with an intensive study of taxation, a topic that is rarely covered much at the undergraduate level. Several of these programs are offered by or jointly with a law school, which means that some or all classes can be similar to law school classes.

Some programs will require the GMAT (or in some cases the GRE) for admissions, but not all do or waive it for work experience or licensure.

It's important to do your research when applying, because not all programs are created equal and a masters in accounting and tax is not a masters in tax. It's not hard to get tricked into applying to one of these suspect graduate programs, since I applied to one program that I thought was a masters in tax that ended up being a masters in accounting and tax with a significantly higher unit requirement than the program I ended up at. Even worse, most of the coursework was duplicative of work I had already done in undergrad.

I started my grad school research by looking at which programs partners and managers on my firm list went to for grad school and then applied to the ones that allowed a part time option. This both allowed me to go to a great school while working but also insured that the master's program had a local reputation so I would able to find a job if necessary. You also want to look at the faculty to see their backgrounds and reputation. In my case, the courses were taught by either partners at accounting or law firms or experienced IRS attorneys and managers. Each of these instructors brought practical and relevant experience in the subject area to the course they were teaching.

Graduate accounting programs.

The final grad school option is a graduate accounting program, often labelled as a master of science in accounting or a masters of professional accountancy. These programs are either intended to provide a qualifying degree or fill a credit deficiency.

I'm not a big fan of these programs unless you need a qualifying degree because many are either a rehash or continuation of undergraduate education. If you have a credit deficiency and are going into tax, you should really go to a graduate tax program instead. However, graduate accounting programs can make sense for some people.

These programs usually require the GMAT (some may accept the GRE). Admission into many programs is based on undergraduate GPA and GMAT score, similar to business school.

The key thing about graduate accounting programs is that you want to look into their alumni network and career services office. It's likely that you'll be going full time and won't be working, so you want to go to a program that will get you hired when you graduate.

You also want to avoid programs that aren't AACSB accredited or have high unit requirements to graduate. Also, watch out for prerequisites as some programs have prerequisites that aren't clear at the outset and will end up significantly increasing your degree cost.

> ## Let's Review:
>
> - ✓ There are multiple options for grad school each of which has pros and cons
> - ✓ Try to avoid going to grad school immediately after undergrad unless you are studying tax or need a qualifying degree
> - ✓ Look into program quality and reputation when picking a grad school program
> - ✓ Beware of undisclosed prerequisites and programs masquerading as something they are not.

Chapter 10: Starting Your Own Practice

Key Concept:

You are in the business of accounting not the accounting business when you start your own practice.

I know that many people probably won't be interested in or read this chapter, since when I talk to student groups about it, it tends to be a very poorly attended meeting. That's not necessarily a bad thing and I don't take it personally, since starting a business is not for everyone. I have several colleagues who would never want to run their own practice or even start a business, just because of the risks of doing so. Their concerns are perfectly reasonable given the fact that many accountants are risk adverse.

I don't want to sugar coat the fact that starting any business is difficult. I know that for me personally launching my practice was one of the most challenging things I've ever done. At the same time, it's also been one of the most rewarding things I've ever done in that it's given me a level of freedom that I've never had before.

I want to start off with discussing why you might not want to start your own practice.

One reason is if you don't like looking for work and aren't able to overcome this dislike, you won't be very successful at running your own practice or even starting a business. As a business owner, your primary responsibility is finding business. Performing the work is secondary to finding the work to perform. Some accountants get lucky and secure a lot of work through one source and stop looking for additional work. The major problem with this is that you are too reliant on this source and are at risk of not making ends meet if the source dries up.

The other reason is if you aren't comfortable with risk. Starting any business is risky because your income is irregular and there is no guarantee of success. If you aren't willing to accept this, then you probably should remain an employee. On the flip side though, there is risk associated with being an employee because you can be laid off or fired. It's just that most people consider the risk associated with being an employee to be less than the risk associated with starting a business.

Now that we've talked about why you might not to start your own practice, let's talk about three reasons why you might want to start a practice.

The first and most significant reason is that you receive the full fruits of your labor. If you work for a firm and get paid $30 per hour, the firm may turn around and bill your time at $150 per hour, a $120 difference. For every hour you work, the firm receives $120 in gross profit. If you run your own firm and bill out at $150 per hour, you get $150 less your business expenses, which will likely mean you will get more than $30.

The second reason is that you control your clients and your schedule. You have the absolute right to choose which clients to serve and when to terminate clients. One of the most frustrating things about working at a firm was dealing with high dollar clients who should be terminated, but had paid the firm too much money that would have to be refunded.

The third reason, which is related to the second, is that you can't be fired. Technology is fundamentally changing accounting and the way accounting services are provided. As a result, the number of accounting jobs will likely decrease over time and the skillset for the remaining jobs will change. Even if this doesn't happen, you are subject to the whims of the employer and their practice management philosophy. I have had some colleagues get "laid off" simply because they were getting paid too much when a younger accountant would be able to do the same work cheaper. As a business owner, the only way you lose your job is if your business fails.

Now that we've discussed why or why not you might want to start your own practice, let's briefly talk about whether it makes sense to do so.

First and foremost, you absolutely must hold a professional license that is valid in the area where you want to practice. If you are planning on becoming a CPA, make sure your work experience is documented before you leave your current firm to avoid issues with your application.

Second, you want to make sure you have support from your immediate family. You're making a difficult decision and lack of support will make it worse.

Third, you need some sort of game plan for your practice that addresses what services you'll provide, how you'll provide them, and to whom.

Fourth and finally, you want to make sure you've eliminated most of your consumer debt and have some savings. If you're forced into business out of necessity, then this becomes less important, but in an ideal world you've eliminated any consumer debt and have a few months in savings.

Once you have these four things covered, then you're ready to open your practice. The key thing is to maximize the launch, because you only get one grand opening, and make sure you're systematic about everything.

The following process is what I would use to relaunch my practice today:

1. Decide where you will be practicing and what an ideal client is.
2. Get a private or virtual office in that area. If you will be in the office a lot, you probably want a private office. If not, a virtual office may work for you. You may also be able to find shared space with other professionals.
3. Get a local phone number through a VOIP provider and an inexpensive answering service that can book appointments for you and an inexpensive online scheduling platform. Some virtual offices will provide a number for you as part of the package, but you don't want to rely on this number. Similarly, you don't want to rely on their staff to book your appointments.

4. Set up a professional looking one page mobile optimized website that focuses on converting leads into prospects.
5. Get errors and omissions insurance. Even if you just buy a cheap tax preparer policy, you want to have insurance because if you screw up, you can't afford to pay the piper
6. Be judicious in spending your money. Keep your expenses low and avoid buying software and stuff unless it's absolutely needed.
7. Join and actively participate in a professional association if you don't already do so.
8. Go where your ideal clients are and reach out to them using language they understand and value and a medium they pay attention to.
9. Spend your down time making new friends and reading books that will help you improve
10. Wow clients with excellent service and cultivate a referral culture.

This ten step process will put you ahead of many other people starting their firm, because you'll be on a vector for success. In addition, keep in mind the following seven maxims for practice management:

1. Always get paid something up front
2. Don't take or keep anything from a prospective client until you are paid.
3. Never sue for fees
4. Consistently fire or sell clients who are a poor fit for your practice and always look for ways to add additional value to current clients. Have no mercy because people don't change. The right client is always right and the wrong client is always wrong.

5. Stay in your lane. If you start doing everything and competing with everyone, you lose out on possible partnerships that make everyone better off.
6. Improve yourself. Leverage your strengths and build your weaknesses
7. Make your business independent of yourself as quickly as possible and scale it once your practice reaches that level. It does you no good to work 80 hours a week for $250,000 a year when you could hire 2 staff members for $100,000 a year, work 10 to 20 hours a week, and make $150,000. This frees you up to find more business.

Now that you have a practice, following these seven maxims will set you up for sustainable growth. Even if you don't want to run a medium sized firm, you will still be able to work smarter and make good money while working reasonable hours.

Let's Review:

- ✓ Not everyone will want to start a practice
- ✓ There are reasons both to start a practice and stay an employee
- ✓ There are risks associated with remaining an employee that should be considered
- ✓ You must be systematic in planning to launch your practice, launching your practice and running your practice

---

DATE: 05 November 2017
TO: Current or Future Accounting Student
FROM: Geoff Plourde, EA, CPA
RE: Closing Thoughts

Congratulations!

You've now made it to the end of this book. As I mentioned in the beginning, I wrote this book to be helpful to students and help them avoid the mistakes I made both during college and coming out of college.

I hope I was successful in doing so and that you found something of value in this book. That being said, I acknowledge that I'm far from perfect and may have missed something or been unclear in parts and welcome your honest review and constructive feedback with improvements or additional information you would like to see in the next edition.

I wish you the best in your academic and professional pursuits.

Sincerely,

Geoff

Geoff Plourde, EA, CPA
geoff@gplourdecpa.com

Appendix A: Suggested Reading

The following is a list of books I recommend. I've broken them into two categories, personal development and business development.

Personal Development

- Getting to Yes, Roger Fisher/William Ury
- How to Win Friends and Influence People, Dale Carnegie
- Linchpin, Seth Godin
- Looking Out for #1, Robert J. Ringer
- Rich Dad, Poor Dad, Robert Kiyosaki
- Seven Habits of Highly Effective People, Steven Covey
- The Greatest Salesman in the World, Og Mandino
- The Richest Man in Babylon, George Clason
- Think and Grow Rich, Napoleon Hill
- Total Money Makeover, Dave Ramsey

Business Development

- 80/20 Sales and Marketing, Perry Marshall
- EntreLeadership, Dave Ramsey
- Managing for Results, Peter Drucker
- Out of the Crisis, W. Edwards Deming
- Scientific Advertising, Claude Hopkins
- The Art of War, Sun Tzu
- The Human Side of Enterprise, Douglas McGregor
- The Millionaire Fastlane, MJ DeMarco
- The New Business Guide, Geoff Plourde
- The Peter Principle, Laurence J. Peter
- The Principles of Scientific Management, F.W. Taylor
- The Pumpkin Plan, Mike Michalowicz
- The Ultimate Marketing Plan, Dan Kennedy
- Up the Organization, Robert Townsend
- Winning through Intimidation, Robert J. Ringer

Appendix B: Cover Letters and Resumes

I know many of you turned here expecting to find samples of cover letters and resumes but I've purposely omitted them from this book for three reasons.

1. There are already many examples on the Internet and your career services webpage
2. I don't want hate mail from your career services office or people who think I'm leading you astray
3. I would rather you understand the point and how to write an effective cover letter and resume.

Resume Advice

Let's start with the resume. The whole point of the resume is to summarize your qualifications and why someone should hire you over the other 99 applicants for the job.

The most valuable thing I can tell you is to make sure your resume looks professional, presentable, and is free of grammatical errors or typos.

Above all, tailor your resume to the requirements of the position and don't be sloppy as this is part of your first and possibly only impression on the hiring manager or partner.

You also should be judicious in what you put on your resume. You have exactly one page of real estate, so make it count and highlight your accomplishments!

Cover Letter Advice

Now let's talk cover letters or emails.

The most important thing here is that you want to write what is called a pain letter (feel free to Google this). No one cares about you, they care about what you will do for them.

Cover emails should be fairly straightforward with a greeting, three paragraphs, and a closing. As I've discussed before, the greeting should always Mr. or Ms. and the recipient's last name. If you can't find the hiring manager's name, then "Hiring Manager" will suffice.

The first paragraph of the cover should answer the following questions:

1. What am I looking for?
2. Why should you hire me/what makes me different?
3. How I know you? (if you've met the person before)

The second paragraph should provide support for the first paragraph that further reinforces the fact that you are what they are looking for.

The third paragraph is the easiest. It will literally just say:

I've included my resume with this email. Should an opportunity be available, I would be most grateful for the opportunity to interview. I can be reached either by email or by phone at xxx.xxx.xxxx.

The closing should simply be:

Sincerely,

Your Name

Wash, rinse, repeat.

Cover letters should look fairly similar, but it is critical that you stick to proper business format. It never ceases to amaze me how many people can't write a business letter. If you are sending a cover letter, it absolutely must be in proper business format.

I've put a sample of proper business format on the next page that I encourage you to look at. Exact formatting may change, but it should look similar to this.

Date

(three lines of space)

Company
Attn: Name
Address
City, State ZIP

(two lines of space)

Dear Mr./Ms. LastName,

I'm writing to show you how to write in proper business format. This paragraph conveys the reason why you are writing and sets the tone for the letter.

The middle paragraphs provide further information about the topic of the letter. Each paragraph corresponds to a topic.

The final paragraph is a closing paragraph that includes formalities like "please don't hesitate to contact me.

Sincerely,

Geoff Plourde, EA, CPA

About the Author

Geoff is the author of *The Automated Accountant*, the *New Business Guide*, the *Small Business Operating Manual* (forthcoming), and the *California Small Business Operating Manual* (forthcoming). His author page can be found on Amazon or on Aptus Press's website at www.aptuspress.com/authors/gplourde.

Geoff currently serves as managing director for the SB Group, a senior advisor to Paragon Business Solutions, and as a consultant for a tax resolution company. He is an enrolled agent and certified public accountant who specializes in resolving complex tax issues and has significant experience working with distressed businesses.

He is an active member of the California Society of Enrolled Agents, San Fernando Valley Chapter and the National Association of Enrolled Agents. He was named a Fellow of the National Tax Practice Institute in 2015 after completing a rigorous program of advanced study in tax problem resolution. He holds a BS in Accounting from Pepperdine University, an MS in Taxation from Golden Gate University, and is a JD candidate at Southwestern Law School.

Geoff started his career at the largest tax resolution firms in the United States, where he represented over 250 businesses and high net worth individuals during his tenure with the firm in tax disputes with the Internal Revenue Service and state taxing authorities.

Geoff can be reached directly by email at geoff@gplourdecpa.com.

Inquiries about this book or other Aptus Press books should be directed to info@aptuspress.com.

www.ingramcontent.com/pod-product-compliance
Lightning Source LLC
Chambersburg PA
CBHW060645210326
41520CB00010B/1749